METAVERSE INVESTING & MARKETI...

Guide to Web 3.0, Non-Fungible Tokens (NFTs) Virtual Real Estate, Games, Development and Future of the metaverse

© COPYRIGHT

TABLE OF CONTENTS

INTRODUCTION

Ever the past year, the idea of "the metaverse" has gained much popularity, and hundreds of projects, both on-chain and off-chain, are attempting to embrace virtual world notions. Many investors are keen to participate in this boom, given that the metaverse niche is anticipated to have a market value of close to $5 trillion by 2030. This book offers a wealth of knowledge on investing in the Metaverse in 2022, outlining numerous common strategies that investors use and the critical considerations when selecting a metaverse platform.

DESCRIPTION

Technology has been advancing and changing quickly. As a result, we are now witnessing advancements that were unthinkable in the past. The Metaverse, a unique, immersive virtual environment swiftly taking over the internet, is one of these developments for many individuals. Though you might have first seen it in science fiction films like Ready Player One or The Matrix series, it is now more accurate than ever.

The Metaverse permeated the internet as virtual reality (VR) and augmented reality (AR) continue to grow. In 2021, it was predicted that 85 million consumers would engage with AR or VR at least once each month. The Metaverse continues to provide incomparably valuable value as a new computing platform, even though it isn't precisely what science fiction imagined.

DEDICATION

Dedicated to all lovers of the metaverse and technology enthusiasts.

CHAPTER 1

What is the Metaverse?

S ome individuals with the haziest understanding of the metaverse may assume it is a video game. In contrast, others may conclude that it is, more broadly speaking, the future of the internet. Both of these theories have some validity, but they only begin to scratch the surface of what the metaverse is all about.

Investors on Facebook are likely aware that the business changed its name to Meta Platforms, a hint to the metaverse. The most straightforward approach to comprehending the metaverse is to consider it a virtual world where people can communicate with one another and the real world.

The word "metaverse" entered everyday speech mainly due to Facebook's name change. However, in 1992, Neal Stephenson is credited with first using the phrase to refer to a fictional, "computer-generated universe" in his book Snow Crash. Given that Facebook wants to have as much power over our lives as possible, it is clear from this description why it would like a piece of the metaverse.

How The Metaverse Functions:

Other businesses besides Facebook had already begun to develop their virtual social worlds. For instance, the online gaming community Roblox has developed a metaverse where users may create and communicate within their games.

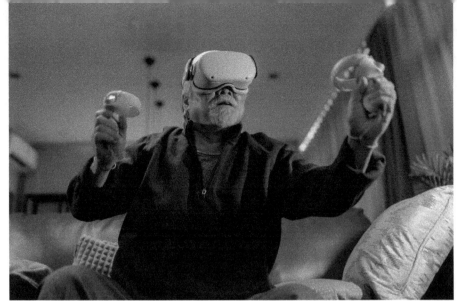

Another example of a metaverse in a video game is Microsoft's Minecraft, albeit a lesser-known example is Microsoft Mesh, which enables connections from a range of devices, including the HoloLens 2, other VR headsets, PCs, and mobile devices.

The metaverse development is anticipated to influence virtual reality (VR) significantly and augmented reality (AR). These instances show that "metaverse" can refer to anything that is both small, like each of these distinct worlds, and huge, like a capitalized "Metaverse," which contains all other metaverses.

Anyone who wants to join any metaverse can log in using any compatible hardware. You are represented online by an avatar when you sign in, which you can customize to suit the latest fashion.

Paying for premium avatar skins or apparel is one possible way that metaverse operators will be able to earn money. In only a few minutes, you may visit virtual storefronts to shop for luxury bags, for example, from the comfort of your couch, according to Colle CEO Akos Balogh. "You are preserving the environment while saving time. In addition, strong communities will develop on a social level since people of all economic backgrounds can access [the metaverse].

If you think that's improbable, you must look at Fortnite to see how much money the game makes from cosmetic things that have no bearing on the character's powers. Epic Games, the company behind Fortnite, is private, so we cannot determine the exact amount of revenue it generates from cosmetic items.

However, it did mention in a presentation early last year that it sold 3.3 million sets of NFL skins in November and December 2018, generating almost $50 million from just that one set of skins in two months. However, it shows how much money these metaverse corporations stand to make from cosmetics. But, of course, some of that money went to the NFL in license fees.

CHAPTER 2

Metaverse Stock

Based merely on how much money they can earn from cosmetics, we've shown that metaverse businesses can be incredibly successful. In what ways might you invest in the metaverse, then? There are a lot of options available to you. Stocks are arguably the most straightforward and straightforward-to-understand way to invest in the metaverse. Meta Platforms is undoubtedly the most popular metaverse stock. Since changing its name, Meta Platforms has introduced the virtual reality metaverse platform Horizon Worlds. Users of Horizon Worlds can connect and play games while exploring the virtual environment using their legless avatars. The company hasn't had much success with its metaverse service. Still, Horizon Workrooms is attempting to make it more accessible to office workers. Ten billion dollars will be spent on metaverse development by Meta Platforms in 2022 alone. These additional equities are in the metaverse:

1. Minecraft and Mesh from Microsoft address the metaverse's game and office/collaboration aspects. The Hololens VR headset is one that Microsoft also makes.
2. Businesses that develop VR hardware may be able to win big in the metaverse. Sony's PlayStation VR and HP's Reverb are a couple of alternatives.

3. Organizations that use cloud computing, such as Amazon Web Services and Microsoft Azure, to manage the back-end infrastructure for the metaverse. Relatedly, Akamai Technologies and Fastly are two potential data centre operators.
4. Roblox is a platform in the metaverse for gamers and anyone who wants to make their games.

5. More than 70% of the top 1,000 mobile games were created using the Unity Software gaming development platform. Additionally, it delivers simulation advancements for a range of sectors. But this business isn't yet lucrative.

6. Matterport, a less popular metaverse player that provides virtual tours for real estate, travel, and hospitality, among other industries.

7. The Omniverse platform from NVIDIA links 3D worlds into a single virtual space. According to the corporation, experts "in a wide array of industries swiftly put it to work."

8. Autodesk creates software engineers and architects use to create structures and goods.

9. Microsoft and Qualcomm are collaborating on their metaverse.

10. Haptic technology, which provides tactile feedback and has several uses in the metaverse, is created by the unnoticed metaverse corporation Immersion Corporation. Then there are the shares of businesses with little to no exposure to the metaverse, such as Nike, which has applied for numerous patents to control the virtual footwear and apparel markets. To increase its production capacities, Boeing is also using the metaverse. With plans to launch its NFT collection and cryptocurrency, even Walmart is covertly laying the groundwork for entering the metaverse. Almost every business that can claim ownership of the metaverse is doing it in some form at the moment because it is such a significant trend.

CHAPTER 3

The Metaverse Real-Estate

Although purchasing stocks in the metaverse may be the most convenient option, you may also purchase real estate there. Owning metaverse real estate allows you to develop it virtually, rent it out, or attempt to sell it for a profit. The non-fungible tokens that make up this digital real estate are produced on blockchain networks to represent some digital assets.

Two of the most well-known metaverse developers, Decentraland and The Sandbox, offer for sale property parcels within their virtual universes. You can profit from creating your virtual property as business owners do in the real world. For instance, Atari constructed its cryptocurrency casino on the 20 parcels it bought on the Decentraland blockchain. In that virtual casino, players may place bets using native ERC20-based tokens from Atari, and tax-free collect their profits in cryptocurrency.

Additionally, the creator of the video game disclosed intentions to construct a digital hotel this year. It is unknown how Atari might generate money from a virtual hotel. Still, when it is made public, the game developer may be able to provide other investors with guidance on how to make money off any virtual real estate they buy.

Like in real life, you can profit from real estate in the metaverse by purchasing it and then reselling it for a profit. For example, an unbelievable $2.5 million was paid for a piece of Decentraland real estate, demonstrating the amount of money that can be made. In the future, it is envisioned that this particular plot of land will contain a sort of fashion district where real-world luxury firms will place advertisements and market digital replicas of their high-end products.

How to Purchase Metaverse Land

Given that each abovementioned metaverse game is based on the Ethereum blockchain, the simplest way to buy a piece of virtual property is through OpenSea. Parcels are unique NFTs that can be exchanged and transferred like any other NFT. The procedure for purchasing an NFT land plot is the same as buying any other NFT.

Connect your cryptocurrency wallet to OpenSea, select the collection and NFT you want to purchase, and then click the large "Buy Now" button to start the transaction. Land can also typically be bought in-game if you want to skip the NFT trading complications and get right into the metaverse.

Decentraland will be used as an example. All you have to do is go to the Decentraland Marketplace to browse and buy land in Decentraland. Find a piece of land within your price range by going to the "Land" section when you arrive there. This entire process will be very familiar if you've ever made an internet purchase. The in-game prompt will lead you through the rest of the transaction process after you locate a parcel and start the buy.

Only ETH or MANA, the local currency of Decentraland, can be used to buy an NFT there. The Sandbox with SAND is similar in this regard. The new token shouldn't intimidate you, though, because getting MANA and SAND is just as simple as getting Fortnite V-Bucks.

That's it after the transaction is finished! You may easily verify that you are now the proud owner of some metaverse real estate by checking your OpenSea account or in-game wallet.

CHAPTER 4

Best Crypto Wallet 2022

Make sure you have a safe and convenient wallet before purchasing Cryptos and making investments in the metaverse. You'll be able to send and receive money quickly and have your crypto tokens stored safely. But first, here is a quick review of the most critical variables you need to take into account:

- -Security and protection
- -Coin transfer and receiving fees
- -A user-friendly user interface
- -Device type, such as hardware, software, or online;
- Additional features, like exchange and swap services

What is a Bitcoin Wallet?

Cryptocurrency wallets come in various forms, each providing a distinct level of security and convenience. A Bitcoin wallet enables you to keep your cryptocurrency investments in their basic form. Your chosen wallet will be connected to the blockchain network, allowing you to transfer and receive tokens at the touch of a button. Mobile wallets, which can be installed on your smartphone via an iOS or Android app, are arguably the most popular storage option. But you can also keep your tokens in a hardware device, online exchange, or desktop program. Additionally, some wallets provide other functions, such as the capacity to purchase, sell, and swap cryptographic assets.

Reasons You Need a Crypto Wallet

The top Bitcoin wallet providers in this market will provide three essential features—storage, sending, and receiving money—. You can't interact with the cryptocurrency markets if you don't have a wallet.

Consider purchasing Bitcoin via credible online exchanges. The exchanger will add the tokens to your online wallet when the transaction is finished. Then, you may choose to transmit the money to a wallet under your control or leave the token on the exchange.

Additionally, if choosing the latter, you must have a private wallet to receive the Bitcoin tokens. This way, cryptocurrency wallets function similarly to a standard checking account. The best cryptocurrency wallets are reviewed below, considering the critical metrics mentioned above.

1. The Best Cryptocurrency Wallet Overall in 2022 is **eToro:**

One of the most fantastic options available in 2022 is eToro if you want to purchase Ethereum, Bitcoin, and other popular altcoins.

The SEC, ASIC, FCA, and CySEC regulate eToro, a well-known cryptocurrency broker. The platform is a top-rated wallet and offers low prices for buying and selling cryptocurrencies. The best combination of security and convenience is provided by eToro, where you may maintain your digital token investments in your account portfolio. When you withdraw your cryptocurrency investments, you can do it instantaneously without having to move tokens between wallets or cryptocurrency exchanges.

As an alternative, you might think about installing the eToro Money Crypto Wallet, which is available as a mobile app. Without sacrificing usability or security, this allows you more control over your digital assets. The eToro Money Crypto Wallet is indeed authorized by the GFSC. Suppose you were to forget your login information or misplace your private keys. In that case, an advantageous feature of eToro Money is that the provider can assist you in regaining access. Additionally, the wallet enables currency exchanges without requiring you to exit the app. You can access brokerage services through eToro's web wallet and mobile wallet. It covers over 500+ cryptocurrency pairs.

You may acquire more than 40 crypto assets for just $10 on a spread-only basis. For instance, you will only need to pay a spread of 2.9% if you wish to purchase Solana. The reach for Axie Infinity will only be 2.9% if you choose to buy it. As a regulated company, eToro accepts deposits and withdrawals in fiat currency. You can add dollars for free as a US

customer using any of the many accepted payment methods, including ACH, debit/credit cards, and e-wallets. Furthermore, eToro provides social and copy trading tools. The former enables you to connect with other eToro investors by commenting on and liking postings. The copy trading tool allows you to replicate a seasoned trader's position precisely. So, with an eToro trading account, you may create a diverse portfolio of stocks, ETFs, cryptos, and more. The best new cryptocurrencies can be purchased from the convenience of your home.

2, **Binance:** The best bitcoin trading app.
Binance dominates the world of cryptocurrencies and blockchain technology. In addition to having the most significant cryptocurrency exchange in terms of trading volume, BNB is a multi-billion dollar crypto asset supported by this exchange.
Binance has a network chain that contains hundreds of decentralized coins. Because of this, Binance is conceivably the most excellent Bitcoin wallet for users looking for both storage and trading options. Many investors will store their tokens in the primary Binance web wallet because it is convenient. You can monitor your investments while on the go by tying the Binance app and the online wallet together.

Both choices are custody wallets, meaning Binance will look after the security of your private keys on your behalf. The Trust Wallet, also supported by Binance, can be downloaded to your smartphone as an alternative. This choice lets you control your private keys and backup passphrase because it is a non-custodial wallet. Please be aware that this implies that Binance will not be able to assist you in regaining access if your wallet is stolen or you misplace your private keys.

ZenGo

But Trust Wallet also grants you access to decentralized programs like Pancakeswap. It gives you access to newly released coins that run on the Binance Smart Chain. As a result, Binance is a beautiful site to purchase well-known altcoins.

3. **ZenGo** – Connect to NFT and Defi Dapps:
A premier NFT wallet, ZenGo is a multi-chain Web3 wallet with many features, such as support for Dapp connections and NFT (non-fungible token) storage.

Its 500,000+ members now span 180 countries after being founded in 2018 and gaining a good reputation in the cryptocurrency business over time. On Google Play and the App Store, which both support Android and iOS, ZenGo has a 4.78/5 rating. ZenGo can be used to connect to preferred gaming Dapps by crypto game enthusiasts.
In addition to storing cryptocurrency, the ZenGo wallet allows for the purchase and exchange of Bitcoin, Ethereum, and other popular cryptocurrencies. Users can also receive a yield of up to 8% on their assets while those cryptocurrencies are safely stored in their wallets. ZenGo offers a simple-to-use recovery kit that can be transferred to new devices if you lose your phone; with 3-factor authentication and 3D biometric encryption, a complex seed phrase is not required.

4. **Coinbase**: The top cryptocurrency wallets for beginners:
Coinbase, which has more than 70 million customer accounts, is similarly responsible for one of the biggest cryptocurrency exchanges on the market to Binance. The platform's services primarily aim at people with little to no experience buying, selling, or keeping digital tokens.

coinbase

Many customers will choose to retain their cryptocurrency holdings in the main Coinbase web wallet, which is jam-packed with security measures. To connect to your Coinbase account, for example, you must first complete two-factor authentication in addition to entering your password.

Furthermore, Coinbase asserts that 98% of all client digital assets are in cold storage. It indicates that the platform maintains a significant portion of its digital currency holdings offline. As a result, a code will be delivered to your smartphone every time you try to log in. The Coinbase wallet also has IP whitelisting as one of its security features. Simply put, this indicates that you will have to pass a second security check if you attempt to log into your account from a new IP address. Even while the Coinbase wallet is user-friendly and secure, we should point out that it isn't the best option for people who want to buy and trade cryptocurrencies. Because regular trading commissions are 1.49%, this is the case. Additionally, this tax rises to 3.99% when paying with a debit or credit card.

5. **Huobi**: Top cryptocurrency interest-earning wallet app:

Although Huobi's primary business is a cryptocurrency exchange, the platform also functions as a web and mobile application. If you choose the first option, you will keep your digital tokens in your primary Huobi account. You won't have access to your private keys. Huobi will instead protect your money and wallet on your behalf. Short-term traders that need immediate access to their digital funds should choose this option. The native Huobi Wallet app, available for both iOS and Android, is the alternative you have. This wallet is not a custodial option like the one on the web.

Huobi

In addition to Bitcoin, Dogecoin, Polkadot, Bitcoin Cash, XRP, EOS, and other tokens, the Huobi Wallet app also supports many different tokens. Once more, this means that you and you alone will be able to access your private keys. As a result, you will continue to have complete control over your crypto tokens. Along with a full range of Defi tokens, the wallet also supports ERC-721 NFTs. The ability to receive interest on cryptocurrency investments through Huobi is arguably the platform's most intriguing feature.
Several variables will affect the exact rate that is due, including the digital asset in issue and whether or not you are willing to lock the tokens away for a particular amount of time.The final cost is a 0.20% commission per slide if you trade on the Huobi exchange.

6. **Trezor** — A Secure Bitcoin Hardware Wallet:
The crypto wallets we have reviewed are available as web storage or mobile apps. Contrarily, Trezor provides a hardware wallet, which means that you will be storing your crypto assets on a real-world gadget.

For those who are not aware, hardware wallets are by far the safest way to keep digital tokens. Hardware wallets like the Trezor are kept offline constantly as a start. Thus, remote hacking attempts are all but impossible as a result of this. Additionally, the PIN you created when you initially set up the device must be physically entered to access the Trezor wallet to send tokens. The timelock feature will start working after a certain number of unsuccessful tries. The amount of time between each subsequent PIN try will therefore double. Therefore, if your Trezor wallet is stolen, you will have time to get your money back from an external device. You can accomplish this by keying in your Trezor backup passphrase on another wallet.

Trezor offers institutional-grade protection for your cryptocurrency investments. Still, if you intend to send and receive money frequently, this choice won't be ideal for you. It is so that you can authorize the transaction, which requires that you have the physical device with you. Last but not least, Trezor is about $85 to purchase.

7. **MetaMask**: The ideal cryptocurrency wallet for Web3 applications:
As the "gateway to blockchain apps," MetaMask claims to be. The wallet works with various cryptocurrency exchanges, NFT marketplaces, play-to-earn cryptocurrency games, and more. Web3 apps, especially those creating applications for decentralized finance, support this wallet to a large extent (Defi).

More than 21 million people use MetaMask, which motivates developers to create new cryptocurrency projects to include support for MetaMask wallets. You alone can access your encryption keys because MetaMask is a self-hosted wallet. The wallet may be installed on iOS and Android devices and natively into Chrome, Firefox, Brave, or Edge web browsers for convenience.

MetaMask features a decentralized exchange that enables token swaps and supports storing any ERC-20 token, including NFTs. The platform is easy to use, but it has a few sophisticated features to help you reduce network fees and ensure you get the best price when trading cryptocurrencies.

8. **Trust Wallet**: An NFT-compatible, user-friendly wallet:
A user-friendly, feature-rich cryptocurrency wallet is Trust Wallet. To begin with, this wallet can perform nearly any task you ask. More than a million different assets are compatible with it, including all ERC-20 tokens, ERC721 NFTs, and ERC1155 NFTs.

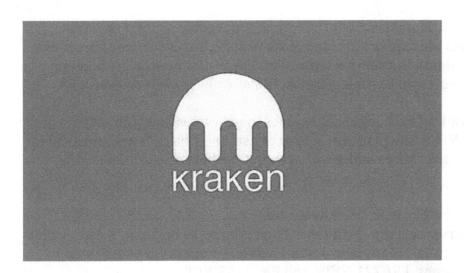

The wallet may connect to more than 53 distinct blockchains in total. Trust Wallet is worth considering if you need a single wallet that can fulfil all possible needs. Trust Wallet additionally enables you to stake your cryptocurrencies to generate interest. Interest rates of up to 11% APY are available when you stake coins like BNB, Kava, Cosmos, Algorand, and Tezos. With Trust Wallet, there are no lock-in times, and the platform doesn't charge a fee for your staking rewards.

Connecting to crypto games, NFT marketplaces, Defi platforms, and other resources is possible. Trust Wallet provides dApps from both Ethereum and Binance Smart Chain. Additionally, Trust Wallet includes a built-in dApps browser that enables you to use this wallet with various Web3 applications.

9. **Kraken**: A Well-Known Crypto Exchange That Also Functions as a Wallet

10. **Electrum** is a fantastic Bitcoin wallet account for holding multiple currencies.

11. **Luno** - Best Bitcoin Wallet for Usability

12. **Exodus**, a free Bitcoin wallet available on both desktop and mobile.

CHAPTER 5

How to Invest In Metaverse:

Those who frequently purchase cryptocurrencies can attest to the metaverse's expansion over the past year, with numerous projects assisting in the general acceptance of this idea. The five tips listed below explain effective ways to invest in the metaverse, and each offers unique advantages to investors:

1. Metaverse Games
2. Metaverse NFTs
3. Metaverse Crypto
4. Metaverse Real Estate
5. Metaverse Stocks

Let's examine the abovementioned strategies in detail and describe how they might help investors in the long run.

Metaverse Games:

We believe the best metaverse investment opportunities are found in the top metaverse NFT projects or in the best metaverse games.

High-profile programs like Decentraland and The Sandbox have driven this game genre to exponential growth over the past year. However, smaller initiatives have frequently been introduced that aim to build on the achievements of those that came before them. In a word, metaverse games are precisely what their name suggests: gaming environments rooted in the metaverse.

These gaming initiatives can function well since many of the top metaverse coins are native to them. The amount of immersion these games can provide players is among their most attractive features. The visuals of metaverse games will be well-known to anyone who has seen Steven Spielberg's "Ready Player One."

They provide gamers with the chance to create their avatars and interact with those of other players in complex 3D worlds. In today's post-pandemic society, this presents a novel means of social interaction that appears destined to spread even further. Play-to-earn (P2E) methods are one of the fascinating aspects for gamers. Through these techniques, players can receive in-game prizes that are valued in cryptocurrencies. In essence, this means that players can profit from their gaming prowess in a fun way.

The metaverse gaming project Battle Infinity has recently attracted media notice. This innovative project includes a fantasy sports league in its metaverse, providing a means for sports lovers to plan and profit from skilful gameplay.

IBAT, the native token of Battle Infinity, is used to disperse these incentives. Due to the project's development potential and other alluring aspects, many investors are interested in purchasing Battle Infinity. One of these is probably the "Battle Store," which offers customers a variety of multiplayer P2E games to play and increases reward possibilities.

Five Leading Metaverse Games:

- Battle Infinity

- Decentraland
- The Sandbox
- Axie Infinity
- Gods Unchained

Metaverse NFTs:

Through NFTs, another well-liked method of investing in the metaverse. The top NFTs from the previous year have been used in projects centred on the metaverse because of their advantageous qualities. The ability to grant "real" ownership of in-game assets is a critical aspect of NFTs that makes them appealing from a metaverse perspective. The in-game playing cards, for instance, are designed as NFTs in the Gods Unchained metaverse game. It ensures that each player's cards are theirs and guards against theft or tampering. In turn, this lessens (or eliminates) the idea of hacking or cheating from the game.

Another advantage is that trading them is simple if in-game things are set up as NFTs. Battle Infinity, which we previously highlighted in the section above, is currently one of the most fantastic NFT projects that offer this feature. Players can purchase, sell, and trade in-game items through the Battle Infinity ecosystem's specialized NFT marketplace (named Battle Market). For instance, users can spend IBAT, the native token of Battle Infinity, to go to the Battle Market and buy a new costume for their in-world avatar.

Since supply and demand determine the price of each NFT, this is yet another choice to invest in the metaverse. NFTs will steadily become more rare and more expensive as the platform's user base expands. Many of the best NFT games, such as Battle Infinity, let players buy virtual pieces of land inside their universe. These games are NFT-structured.

Most Popular Metaverse NFTs:

- Battle Infinity
- Gods Unchained,
- Gods Unchained,
- Decentraland
- Axie Infinity

Metaverse Cryptocurrency:

Using metaverse cryptocurrency is an additional method of investing in the metaverse. In a nutshell, "metaverse crypto" refers to the native tokens of projects built in the metaverse. These tokens are frequently utilized for many purposes, including transactions, staking, and governance. Let's examine these in greater detail:

In-world transactions:

Typically, the native token of each metaverse can be used to make purchases from the in-world market. Users can purchase Axie Infinity, for instance, and then use tokens to buy more 'Axies' in the game. It also means that vendors are paid in metaverse cryptocurrency, which they may later convert into another kind of digital money.

Staking:
To increase the network's security, crypto staking entails "locking up" tokens for a predetermined time. Numerous metaverse platforms provide a staking feature that enables token holders to earn a return on their investments while also helping the wider community.

Governance:
Last but not least, many metaverse initiatives have a decentralized autonomous organization (DAO) structure, which means that the platform's token holders control it. The majority of the best crypto DAO initiatives let token holders vote on proposed changes to the governance model; the proposals with the most votes are implemented. Because there are several uses for metaverse cryptocurrency, the list above is not all-inclusive.

They also offer a simple way to invest in the metaverse because they are frequently listed on the top cryptocurrency exchanges. Because of this, investing in tokens allows investors who aren't engaged in a particular metaverse to benefit from its expansion. Axie Infinity is an excellent example since AXS tokens were valued at more than $164 in November 2021. When MANA tokens soared over 110% earlier in the year, investors who chose to purchase Decentraland were likewise richly rewarded. Finally, anyone interested in making a metaverse investment can buy IBAT tokens during the Battle Infinity presale to get a piece of the project's future growth.

Top 5 Crypto Assets In The Metaverse:

- Axie Infinity
- Ethereum
- Decentraland
- Battle Infinity
- Enjin

Real Estate in the Metaverse:

With its distinctive perspective on ownership and renting, metaverse real estate has emerged as one of this expanding industry's most fascinating components. Those interested in investing to invest in metaverse real estate can do so by participating in metaverse projects that let consumers buy virtual land plots.

Given that its 3D environment has almost 90,000 plots of 16m x 16m land parcels, Decentraland is one of the most notable projects that provide this feature (called LAND). LAND, which features an NFT structure, may be bought with Ethereum or MANA (Decentraland's native token). Metaverse real estate can be expensive in some situations, given that these plots are just 16m x 16m in size. Like in real life, specific land plots are valued more than others due to their location. Even in 2021, the value of some of the LAND plots next to "Genesis Plaza" in Decentraland exceeded $13,000.

In 2021, virtual land sales in the metaverse were expected to reach $500 million, according to a CNBC story. The advantages that investing in virtual real estate can provide investors have been primarily responsible for this. Investors can profit from value growth fueled by an increase in the project's popularity and rental income.

Renting operates precisely as one might anticipate, enabling virtual landowners to charge others a fee to use their property. This is accomplished using virtual billboards, which can be purchased via IBAT. Users can lease land from others and then use it for advertising in Battle Infinity's "Battle Arena," which incorporates this system. Since this "land" is still only a collection of pixels within a 3D universe, investors looking to buy metaverse real estate must ensure the property has intrinsic worth. However, making wise investments in this field can pay off, as numerous NFT land ventures have demonstrated.

Most Promising Metaverse Real Estate Projects:

- Decentraland
- Battle Infinity
- The Sandbox
- Somnium Space

- Meta Mansions

Metaverse Stocks:

Investors who want to trade on the equities market rather than the cryptocurrency sector may find a wide variety of metaverse stocks to invest in appealing. The finest metaverse equities might not provide "direct" exposure to the development of a particular platform but the development of the sector as a whole.

Finding metaverse businesses to invest in makes it simple to diversify a portfolio and avoid becoming "overexposed" to one project. One excellent example is Meta Platforms, which was initially Facebook and is now heavily invested in virtual reality (VR) and the development of metaverse ideas. Since Nvidia chips now power numerous metaverse initiatives, the company is a preferred choice.

Naturally, the growth of the metaverse and the need for Nvidia's chips in more projects will boost the company's earnings and stock price. The metaverse is home to some of the most undervalued equities. Many well-known companies are trying to test concepts connected to virtual worlds.

As a result of the company's partnership deals with Decentraland and Roblox to increase its footprint in this space, Nike has emerged as one of the top metaverse stocks to invest in. In the end, buying metaverse stocks can be a terrific method to direct investment in the industry's expansion while also getting indirect exposure to a specific project.

This strategy may be better suited for market beginners because buying equities is more straightforward than buying cryptocurrency.

Top 5 Metaverse Stocks

- Meta-Platforms
- Nvidia
- Nike
- Coinbase
- Roblox

CHAPTER 6

How to Spot Best Metaverse Projects

Like finding the finest altcoins, finding the best metaverse projects with the most promise may be done in several ways. Some of the more well-liked methods are listed below:

1. Pick Trending New Assets Like Battle Infinity:

Finding new and upcoming projects to invest in is one of the most popular strategies employed by metaverse investors. These projects frequently borrow ideas from earlier works and give them their distinctive twist, precisely what Battle Infinity intends to do. Battle Infinity has already been covered, but this new metaverse project is the best option for investors. A broad audience will enjoy Battle Infinity's token rewards system. Fans of football, cricket, basketball, the NHL, and other sports will love its fantasy sports league. Due to these features, this project is being hailed as one of the most exciting of the year.

2. Think About Businesses In The Metaverse:

The equity market still offers lucrative investments for those who prefer stocks to cryptocurrency. It is expected to grow in the years to come. As previously mentioned, many non-crypto organizations utilize metaverse concepts in their business operations. We would anticipate that more businesses would employ this strategy to enhance the customer experience—and their profits—given the opportunity for consumer participation offered by the metaverse.

3. Look for Passive Income Potential:

Crypto staking is a standard method for market players to earn passive income in cryptocurrency. Various metaverse ventures are now using this strategy (including Battle Infinity). Selecting metaverse projects with the potential for passive income can be a terrific method to provide a dividend while enjoying price appreciation.
Users can also make a regular income by playing play-to-earn (P2E) games despite being slightly more "active." These games award token rewards for displaying expertise that can be exchanged for other currencies and used to buy products and services.

4. Social media utilization:

The usage of social media channels by many leading projects in the cryptocurrency market has allowed them to reach a sizable audience of retail investors. Real-time information on innovative and fascinating initiatives has also been found on websites like Twitter and Reddit.

Additionally, these forums frequently contain a balanced conversation, allowing potential investors to see a project's positive and negative aspects.

5. Take a look at the white paper:
Finally, by reading the whitepaper and roadmap of high-potential metaverse projects, investors can make a choice. These two components are critical to the sustainability of a project because they essentially inform investors of what to anticipate in the months and years to come. A project with a vital whitepaper and a clear roadmap are typically good indicators of its potential for a valuable project.

CHAPTER 7

Marketing in the Metaverse

D igital marketers must stay current with new technological advancements. How do marketers adjust as the metaverse gets bigger? First, marketers must remember how valuable millennials and Gen Z consumers are as a target market. With this in mind, let's investigate how marketing can be done in the metaverse.

What Is Achievable With Metaverse Marketing?

Instead of merely posting conventional ads, provide interactive brand installations and events. Capitalizing on metaverses' sensory and immersive character is advisable to provide the exact immersive experience in your marketing and advertising campaigns.
A Lil Nas X performance on Roblox, visits to the Gucci Garden, and a virtual recreation of the Washington Heights neighbourhood created as part of Warner Bros.' Recently, brands have discovered new sources of income by working with the Roblox metaverse and other metaverses.

Is Metaverse the Future?

Many businesses are now making investments in metaverses. They are placing bets on it for business, professional, and fun. Building social metaverses and investing in Oculus, Facebook's AR and VR technologies, are Mark Zuckerberg's main priorities. For instance, Facebook, the most popular social media site, envisions itself as a metaverse business in the future. For Oculus, Zuckerberg unveiled a work metaverse in August 2021 that enables individuals to collaborate, sit in a conference room, and communicate as if in an office.
This is timely given that more offices are implementing work-from-home policies. Silicon Valley has been actively investing in metaverses as the next wave of the internet, more than just Facebook. There are now several games that have metaverse-like components on their platforms. For instance, the video games Animal Crossing and Fortnite both support concerts.

In addition, HTC is focusing on developing VR technologies for businesses rather than consumers. It shows that VR technology is gradually moving beyond entertainment. If the information mentioned above wasn't enough to persuade you, perhaps this will: people purchase real estate in the metaverse, especially on Earth 2. That alone is a clear sign that the technology is here to stay.

Why Brands Are Marketing In The Metaverse:

Marketers are swarming to the metaverse for a variety of reasons. It's new, and there are quick connections to handle expanding environments. The fact that marketers can target Millennials and Gen X in new ways thanks to metaverses is perhaps the most crucial factor. Marketers want to reach these audiences and keep them informed about and interested in their products and technologies. It is also evident from the level of interaction brands are already experiencing that this marketing approach is practical and here to stay.

Because they are located in the digital world, the largest metaverses, like Fortnight and Roblox, present large businesses with previously unachievable opportunities. Verify Vans. According to The Wall Street Journal, the skateboarding company has introduced a virtual skatepark in Roblox where users can try out new tricks and earn points to decorate their avatars in the store.

According to the Vans executive team, the ideal area to increase brand recognition among their target market of 13 to 35-year-olds is the internet metaverse. The company claims more than 48 million people have visited their online park. Larger companies with more considerable funds can observe that kind of interaction in the metaverse. Gucci joined the fray as well. The Gucci Virtual 25 is an exclusive digital pair of sneakers that the luxury company unveiled in March 2021, according to The Verge, and that "can be 'worn' in augmented reality (AR) or utilized in connected applications like Roblox and VRChat." Even though they are merely virtual items, they sell for $12.99 on the platforms, which is reasonable for a piece of abundant clothing. They were very astute, but they didn't stop there.

Gucci launched the Gucci Garden on Roblox in May 2021 as a virtual experience to go along with the Gucci Garden Archetypes. This physical exhibit took place in Florence, Italy. People might "mix with others exploring the room and can buy digital artefacts produced in conjunction with Roblox creator Rook Vanguard," according to Vogue Business. These two partnerships illustrate how brands can be far more inventive online than they can in the real world. In addition, a larger and far more active audience.

How Brands Can Participate in the Game:

There are starting to be more frequently emerging non-gaming metaverses. Conventions are now happening virtually in the metaverse. Attendees don't need to leave their offices or homes to see a lot of exhibitors. When you bring the experience online, the audience size increases tremendously. Consider the potential audience for automobile shows in the metaverse. To experience and observe a car from the inside out, put on some virtual reality goggles and "sit" in one. These events have a lot of creative potentials. Because branding, marketing, and advertising in the metaverse are so new, the costs to run a campaign are still relatively minimal. It's time to try it if you're a brand or company with an open mind and your target audience frequents the metaverse.

Remember that conventional advertising won't work; you'll need to be inventive and use interaction as your primary KPI. The measuring and tracking we're used to with other marketing methods aren't available because this technology is new. Still, it won't be long before the analytics catch up.

CHAPTER 8

Obstacles in the Metaverse:

There are still some obstacles to overcome on the road to the beautiful future that the metaverse promises for brands. Accessibility is a problem for metaverses due to the technological constraints they face. One is that, although metaverses are becoming more and more common, they still require incredible support. Not everyone has access to tools like high-end computers and VR glasses that are required to enjoy the metaverse. It severely restricts the potential market for brands and makes mass marketing efforts difficult. When traversing metaverses, brands also need to be cautious. To avoid turning investors against the brand, seamless integration is essential. Since the technology is still in its infancy, brands may still have problems establishing their rightful position in the metaverse and may appear overly direct in their messaging. Plan your locations carefully, and make sure the metaverse feels natural and well-integrated. Metaverses continue to be the subject of many misconceptions. They are frequently considered to be a simple kid's game. Brands attempting to develop a presence within metaverses risk their efforts not being taken seriously because not everyone appreciates the usefulness of these platforms.

The metaverse still faces problems with data security and privacy. More sophisticated security measures are required as a result of new technology. This necessitates creating brand-new data privacy and protection techniques when none previously existed. Personal verification, for instance, can demand more information from users, raising concerns about data privacy. Last but not least, since metaverses are open to anyone, brands must take care to safeguard their reputation.

Your brand is more likely to be associated with dubious content the more control people have over the metaverse. Additionally, you risk having users insult or vandalize your placements. Since customers want to feel comfortable interacting with you in the virtual world, your marketing methods must be fluid, thoughtful, and exact.

CONCLUSION

Investment in the metaverse can be profitable, especially given that by 2030 it is anticipated that the market would be worth close to $5 trillion. There are various easily accessible ways to obtain exposure to this growth, as this guide has demonstrated, ensuring that all sorts of investors have a choice. Whichever project backers decide to support, it's easiest to do so using the top Metaverse apps.

This book frequently brings up the Battle Infinity project, and with good cause. Recently launched, this project is now in a presale stage where interested parties can buy tokens at a discount. This could be a fantastic chance for anyone hoping to profit from the metaverse's expansion, given the success that past presales have had in the metaverse market.